Published by

WELLTON BOOKS
P.O. Box 6066
Folsom, CA 95630

Written and illustrated by
Debbie and Stephen Cornwell

—Printed in the U.S.A.—

CAUTION! . . . this book is intended for lovers and potential lovers! Excessive use of our romantic recipes may result in loss of sleep. We suggest you reserve these menus for only your most special and playful occasions!

Remember that attitude and ambiance are primary ingredients to seductive dining. Be sure you understand the importance of **"Before Play"** and the risk of **"Cheap Frills"** <u>before</u> you try the first recipe!

To enjoy each dining experience to its' fullest, approach every recipe as the beginning of a new and uniquely exciting evening of seduction. Take the time to entice your companion with an **"Appeteaser"** before you offer the **"Piece de no Resistance"**! We've provided specific menu recommendations for each entrée, but, you'll note that we seldom make mention of desserts . . . how you conclude each evening of dining is left totally to your imagination!

CONTENTS

CHEAP FRILLS

(Creating the Mood)

Creating an atmosphere of intimacy and intrigue will captivate your intended lover even before the first course is served. The tactics which you employ will depend on your personality and intentions. Is your heart's desire a new acquaintance, your spouse, or something in between? If your companion is familiar with your environment and style of dining, creating the mood may involve a change in both. If the relationship is already intimate, what would you do differently if this were the evening of first seduction? Get the picture? Sure you do! Lusty thoughts, everything special, setting the mood to realize your fantasy.

And it doesn't take that much effort to tablecloth the table, accent your setting with fresh flowers, and to lower the lighting. A dimmer switch is a great cheap frill!

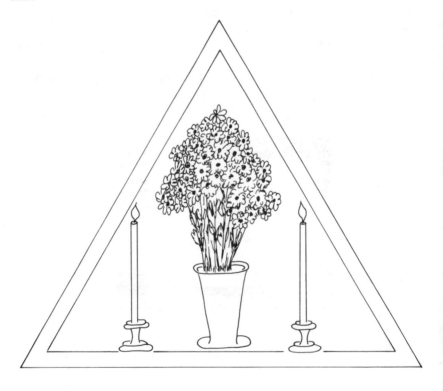

Your next step should be an excursion in self-expression. Table linens reflect your moods and can provide a very subtle, yet unmistakable, suggestion to your companion. Start with a solid color tablecloth. For versatility, buy several sets of napkins. Choose your patterns to best express your playful personality. For example:

—an amorous and sultry tropical print in deliciously deep rich colors conveys an aura of clandestine intrigue

—a sporty adventurous print in bright, vivid, spirited colors and patterns will portray you as bold and confident.

To complete your seductive scenario, add fresh flowers, candlelight and, plan your selection of music for the evening (television is very counter productive to seduction). Don't forget the obvious either...turn on the answering machine, make arrangements for the kids (if any) for the evening and, tell your best friend you're out of town!

You've paid attention to every delectable detail in creating the mood. The ambiance is perfect and you still have an hour before the object of your affection will be served the first course. You can relax now, take a deep breath, and reflect on the romantic rewards you're soon to reap!

DOES SIZE REALLY MATTER?

(PRESENTATION)

It has probably been debated since Adam first cooked for Eve, however, it most definitely matters when it comes to an appropriate selection of serving pieces and stemware. Au gratin dishes are recommended for many of our recipes . . . the 9″ size is superb for entrees, while the 5″ is perfect for something on the side. An assortment of either ramekins, pedestal dessert dishes or small bowls is also a must for proper presentation of individual sauces, dressings, and condiments. Now we're not suggesting you throw away your everyday dishes or pull the china out of the closet — just add some variety to what you usually use and keep the mayonnaise jar off the table. Play the best shot your pocketbook can afford and remember your objective!

BEFORE PLAY

(Pantry Needs)

Your pantry must become the catalyst for adventurous dining endeavors. Each recipe which follows will include its own suggestions for seasonings and garnishes. Tailor them to your own tastes and experiment. Do not be afraid to take culinary license. Explore all possibilities and give in to whimsey! (Nothing ventured, nothing gained!) A well-stocked pantry, including the following list of seasonings and garnishes, will allow you the versatility to prepare all our recipes.

anchovy fillets
artichoke hearts, marinated
artichoke hearts, waterpacked
canned diced chilis
capers
cashews
fresh chives
fresh dill
fresh ginger
fresh jalapenos
fresh parsley
lemons
limes
oyster sauce
peanuts
pecans
pine nuts
pistachios
Rafetto Chut-Nut chutney
slivered almonds

basil
bay leaves
cayenne
chervil
curry powder
Dijon style mustard
ginger
hot mustard
liquid smoke
marjoram
nutmeg
oregano
paprika
tarragon
Tobasco sauce
Worcestershire sauce

brandy
dry sherry
dry white wine
Triple Sec
Madiera
Port
Rum

GRATIN OF CRAB

40 Minutes

STEP ONE

1/2 C. milk
one half jalapeno chili, minced
1/2 t. thyme
1 bay leaf
1 t. parsley, minced
salt and pepper to taste
1 C. soft bread crumbs
1/2 lb. crabmeat, patted dry

Combine milk, chili, herbs and seasonings in small saucepan over medium-high flame and bring to a boil. Reduce heat and simmer 10 minutes. Strain into bowl, add bread crumbs, set aside 10 minutes.

STEP TWO

3 slices bacon, cut into 1/2 pieces
1 1/2 T. green onion, sliced
one half jalapeno chili, minced
1 1/2 T. snipped chives
1 1/2 T. parsley, minced
1/2 t. thyme
1/2 t basil

Fry bacon, onion, and chilies until bacon is crisp. Remove and drain on paper towels. In large bowl, combine bacon mixture and herbs. Squeeze bread crumbs dry and mix into bacon mixture. Fold in crab.

STEP THREE

2 T. butter
4 t. fresh lime juice
1 T. rum
2 T. finely grated Gruyere cheese
1/2 avocado, sliced
lime wedges

Preheat oven to 325°. In large frypan over medium flame, saute' crab mixture until browned. Blend in lime juice and rum. Butter two small scallop shells or individual baking dishes. Mound crab mixture in center of each and sprinkle with cheese. Place on baking sheet and bake 10 minutes. Garnish with avocado slices and lime wedges. Serve immediately.

ARTICHOKE BALLS

30 Minutes

STEP ONE

1 6 oz. jar marinated artichoke
    hearts drained, reserve
    marinade
4 (waterpacked) artichoke hearts,
    drained
2 eggs
1 large clove garlic, minced
2 t. Worcestershire
1/4 t. Tobasco
1/4 t. liquid smoke
1 C. Italian bread crumbs
3/4 C. Parmesan

Mince artichoke hearts and set aside. Beat eggs with 2 T. marinade. Add garlic, Worcestershire, liquid smoke and Tobasco, blend well. Add artichokes and bread crumbs. Form into 1 inch balls and roll in Parmesan. Place on lightly greased baking sheet, cover and chill until ready to serve. (Best if left several hours to allow flavors to blend.) Bake at 325° for 7 - 10 minutes.

STUFFED GRAPE LEAVES

1 Hour 20 Minutes*

STEP ONE

6 dried apricots
2 T. walnuts, coarsely chopped
1/4 lb. ground lamb
3 T. raw rice
1 green onion, chopped
2 t. snipped chives
1/8 t. cinnamon

Combine first seven ingredients in bowl, mix well. Lay grape leaf, veins up, stem toward you. Place 1 tablespoon of filling at base of leaf, roll, tucking sides in neatly. Place seam side down in 3 qt. saucepan. Repeat. Sprinkle with lemon juice, cover with water bring to a boil. turn flame to low, cover, simmer 1 hour.*

STEP TWO

1 jar grape leave, rinsed, patted dry
1 T. lemon juice
mint jelly
current jelly

Remove grape leaves from pan, cool slightly. Place unused grape leaf on salad plate, top with 3-4 stuffed grape leaves. Put a dollop of mint jelly on one side and a dollop of currant jelly on the other. Serve.

CRAB AND SHRIMP DUET

2 Hours, 30 Minutes*

STEP ONE

1/4 t. paprika
3 T. olive oil
1 - 2 anchovy fillets, mashed
1 t. Dijon style mustard
1 t. lemon juice
1/3 C. celery, tender center ribs,
    sliced
2 T. parsley, minced
1 T. chives, snipped

Whisk paprika, oil, anchovies, mustard, and lemon juice together until well blended. Add celery, parsley and chives and blend thoroughly.

STEP TWO

1 C. medium shrimp, cooked,
    shelled and deveined
1 C. crabmeat, cooked
lettuce leaves (red leaf, butter
    lettuce or iceberg)
1 T. parsley, chopped

Toss shrimp with dressing to coat. Gently fold in crab. Cover and marinate 2 hours* in refrigerator. Let stand at room temperature for 30 minutes prior to serving. Place lettuce leaves on chilled salad plates. Mound crab and shrimp mixture in center and garnish with a sprinkle of parsley.

LETTUCE BE LOVERS

Your salad should be an extension of your uninhibited spirit. We encourage you to show a bit of daring in your dressing by departing from the usual vinaigrettes or creamy whatevers! An innovative composition of greens and garnishes, served with a unique dressing will reflect your confidence in the evening. Our avocado based dressing is boldly different in appearance, yet mild enough to compliment the most delicately flavored entrée.

Avocado Dressing

½ avocado
¼ C. sour cream
3 T. whipping cream
½ t. garlic, minced
1 T. plain yogurt
1 T. red wine vinegar
½ t. salt
1-2 dash Tobasco sauce

Combine all ingredients in blender and blend until smooth. Thin with more whipping cream, if necessary.

Gratin of Crab

Deep Six Salad

Fantasies

au Fruits du Mer

Sauvignon Blanc

FANTASIES AU FRUITS DE MER

Ancient mariners have long held fantasies of the deep. To what depths do your fantasies go?

30 Minutes

STEP ONE

1/2 C. olive oil
1 clove garlic, minced
1/4 C. lemon juice
8 - 10 drops Tobasco sauce
1/4 C. chopped fresh dill
2 T. chopped leek
3 T. fresh chopped parsley
1 t. fresh ground pepper
1/2 C. ham cut into julienne
    strips
1/2 C. frozen petite peas
2 small firm tomatoes,
    chopped

Combine all ingredients, except ham and peas, in large bowl. Mix thoroughly. Fold in ham and peas.

STEP TWO

1/2 lb. fresh ocean scallops
1/2 lb. fresh shrimp, peeled,
    deveined

Boil water. Drop shrimp in and cook 1 minute, or until pink. Remove immediately and add to dressing. Drop in scallops, stir until almost opaque, remove and add to dressing.

STEP THREE

6 - 8 oz. fettucini, cooked
1/4 C. chopped pistachio nuts

Add fettucini, toss, spoon into warmed au gratin dishes, top with pistachios and serve immediately.

PEEL ME A GRAPE

We couldn't remember if this was what Cleopatra said to Marc Anthony or if Mae West coined the phrase. We are sure that whoever said it knew what they were suggesting!

25 Minutes

STEP ONE

2 T. oil
2 T. butter
3/4 lb. fresh ocean scallops, quartered
1 C. seedless green grapes

Heat butter and oil over medium flame. Add scallops and grapes and sauté until scallops become opaque, about 2 minutes. Transfer scallops and grapes to bowl.

STEP TWO

2 large leeks, chopped
2 cloves garlic, minced
10 mushrooms, sliced
1 t. basil
3/4 t. tarragon
1/2 t. thyme
1/2 t. chervil
2 T. flour
3/4 C. dry white wine
1/2 t. sugar
1/2 C. whipping cream
salt and pepper, to taste

Add leeks to pan and sauté until limp. Add garlic, mushrooms and herbs, continue cooking 5 minutes. Whisk in flour. Add wine, whisk until sauce is thickened, then add cream and sugar. Continue whisking until sauce is thickened. Return scallops and grapes to pan, stirring gently to coat with sauce.

STEP THREE

6 - 8 oz. cooked linguine
1/2 avocado, cut to bite size pieces

Turn linguine into warmed au gratins, spoon sauce over and sprinkle with avocado pieces.

Artichoke Balls

Lusty Leaves

Peel Me A Grape

Pistachio Carrots

Fumé Blanc

Artichoke Balls

Calypso Salad

Sea Nymph Promise

Vegetable Sauté

Fumé Blanc

SEA NYMPH PROMISE

Greek legend has it that a sea nymph, Calypso, promised her lovers immortality if they would never leave her. You of course, should negotiate your own terms!

25 Minutes

STEP ONE

3 T. butter
1 leek, chopped
6 mushrooms, sliced
2 T. fresh parsley, minced
1 large tomato, chopped
1/2 t. oregano
salt and pepper, to taste
2 T. sherry

Melt butter in saucepan over medium flame. Add leek, parsley and mushrooms, stirring until they are soft. Add tomato and seasonings, simmer until reduced by half. Blend in sherry, turn flame to high and boil 2 minutes.

STEP TWO

3 T. butter
2 cloves garlic, minced
3/4 lb. medium shrimp, peeled and deveined
4 oz. feta cheese, crumbled
2 T. parsley, chopped

In large frypan, over medium flame, melt butter. Add garlic and stir for 30 seconds to release its aroma. Add shrimp and stir until pink. Bring tomato mixture to a boil, add shrimp mixture and 3 oz. feta cheese. Heat through. Spoon into warmed au gratin dishes. Garnish with remaining feta and parsley.

SQUEEZE ME!!!

Lime in the mood for love!

40 Minutes

STEP ONE

1 T. olive oil
2 celery ribs, sliced
1 leek, chopped
1 C. fish stock
2 firm tomatoes, chopped
1 4 oz. can diced green chilies
    (med. hot)
2 T. fresh lime juice
2 T. fresh parsley, chopped
2 green onions, sliced
1 clove garlic, minced
2 T. white wine
1/4 t. basil
1/2 t. fresh ground black pepper

In large frypan, heat oil over medium flame. Add celery and leek, cover and cook until soft. Remove cover, turn flame to high and add stock, tomatoes, chilies, lime juice, parsley, onion, garlic, wine, basil and pepper. Bring to a boil, reduce heat and simmer 15 minutes.

STEP TWO

2 large fresh orange roughy fillets
parsley sprigs
lime wedges

Add fish to sauce and continue to simmer 20 minutes longer (or until fish is opaque). Gently, remove fish to warmed au gratins, ladle sauce over fish, garnish with parsley and lime wedges. Serve immediately.

Stuffed Grape Leaves

Temptation Salad

Squeeze Me

Pistachio Carrots

Chardonnay

Shrimp & Crab Duet

Alluring Leaves

Coy Catch

Carrot Potato Au Gratin

Chardonnay

A COY CATCH

Don't let the best one get away!

40 Minutes

STEP ONE

4 T. butter
2 snapper fillets, patted dry
salt and pepper, to taste
1/4 C. flour

Preheat oven to 400°. Butter a flame-proof baking dish. In large frypan, over medium flame, melt butter. Combine salt, pepper and flour in plastic bag, add snapper and shake to coat. Add snapper to pan and brown on both sides. Remove to baking dish.

STEP TWO

1/4 C. onion, minced
3/4 C. white wine
3/4 t. chervil
1/2 t. tarragon
1 t. basil
1 T. fresh parsley, minced
1 T. fresh snipped chives (3/4 t. dry chives)
3/4 C. whipping cream
paprika

Turn flame to low, add onion, saute' until limp. Add wine to pan, turn flame to high and boil. Add chervil, tarragon, basil, parsley, chives and cream. Season with salt and pepper. Pour over snapper and bake until it is opaque (about 8 minutes) baste occasionally. Transfer snapper to heated plates. Place baking dish over high flame, bring to a boil and reduce liquid by half. Pour over snapper, dust with paprika and serve.

FLIRTATIOUS FILLETS

Flirting can pay and go a long way . . . just be prepared to roll in the hay!

35 Minutes

STEP ONE

1/2 C. dry white wine 1/2 C. whipping cream 2 T. minced leek 1 C. butter 6 radishes, minced 2 T. fresh chopped dill 1 T. prepared horseradish salt, to taste 1/4 t. white pepper	To saucepan over medium flame, add wine, cream and leek. Bring to a boil, stirring, until reduced by half. Turn flame to low, and whisk in butter, 2 tablespoons at a time. Stir in radishes, dill, horseradish, salt and pepper. Turn flame off.

STEP TWO

2 salmon fillets 1/2 C. milk 1/3 C. flour 1 T. butter 1 T. olive oil 2 radishes, thinly sliced 2 sprigs dill	Pour milk into pie pan. Put flour in another pie pan. Melt butter and oil in frypan over medium flame. Dip salmon in milk, then in flour. Add salmon to pan and saute until golden brown. Turn and repeat until salmon is opaque. Ladle a little sauce into warmed au gratins. Top with salmon, nap salmon with sauce, arrange radish slices and dill as garnish. Serve immediately.

Cheese Crock

Impetuous Leaves

Flirtatious Fillets

Artichoke Fromage

Sauvignon Blanc

Artichoke Balls

Got'cha Greens

Chicken Aphrodesia

Vegetable Sauté   Chardonnay

CHICKEN APHRODESIA

Gives the rooster a booster and the chicken a delight!

1 Hour

STEP ONE

1/2 C. butter
1 C. onion, chopped
2 cloves garlic, minced
2 red potatoes, peeled, cut in
    1/2" cubes
1 C. ham, cut in 1/2" cubes
1 C. fresh mushrooms, sliced
1/2 C. white wine
1 T. parsley, minced

Melt butter in large frypan over medium flame. Add onion, leek, garlic and potatoes. Saute' for 15 minutes or until golden brown. Add ham, mushrooms, wine, 1 leek, chopped, and parsley. Continue cooking until mushrooms are giving up their juices. Spoon mixture into ovenproof serving dish. Cover and keep warm in 200° oven.

STEP TWO

3/4 C. flour
1 t. salt
1/2 t. fresh ground pepper
1/4 t. cayenne
1 chicken breast, boned, skinned,
    cut in 1" x 1 1/2"
2 chicken legs, boned, skinned,
    cut in 1" x 1 1/2" strips

Combine flour, salt, pepper and cayenne in plastic bag. Add chicken strips in batches, shake to coat. Add 3 T. oil to pan and saute' chicken until golden brown, drain on paper towels. Arrange on top of vegetable mixture, cover and return to oven.

STEP THREE

1 1/2 T. minced leek
1/4 t. garlic, minced
2 t. lemon juice
1/3 C. white wine
1 1/2 t. chervil
1 1/2 t. tarragon
1/4 t. white pepper

Combine all ingredients and cook over medium flame until reduced to 3 T.

STEP FOUR

3 large egg yolks
1/8 t. cayenne
1/3 C. white wine
1/2 C. butter, melted

Put wine, eggs and cayenne in blender, mix 2 seconds, add reduced herb mixture, turn on high speed and add butter in slow stream until mixture is thickened slightly. Pour over chicken and serve.

A LITTLE DILL WILL DO!

It isn't how much you use, it's how you use it!

30 Minutes

STEP ONE

2 T. butter
1 T. lemon juice
1 clove garlic, minced
1/8 t. white pepper
1/4 t. paprika
2 T. fresh dill, chopped
10 - 12 button mushroom caps
3 T. dry white wine
2 chicken breasts, boned and
    skinned

Melt butter in frypan over medium flame. Add lemon juice, garlic, pepper, paprika, dill, mushrooms and wine. Bring just to boiling point, turn flame to low. Add chicken, turning to coat, cover and simmer 20 minutes.

STEP TWO

1 T. flour
1/2 C. whipping cream
dill sprigs

Remove chicken to warm au gratin dishes. Whisk flour into wine sauce. Cook, whisking constantly, 2 minutes. Blend in cream and warm through. Nap chicken with sauce and garnish with fresh dill sprigs. Serve immediately.

Shrimp & Crab Duet

Suggestive Salad

A Little Dill Will Do

Carrot Potato Au Gratin

Chenin Blanc

Gratin of Crab

Adventurous Greens

Exotic Erotic Chicken

Carrot Potato Au Gratin

Chardonnay

EXOTIC EROTIC CHICKEN

Set the trap with exotic bait and erotic game may be your catch!

1 Hour, 30 Minutes

STEP ONE

2 T. butter
1/2 C. flour
1 t. paprika
1/8 t. cayenne
1/8 t. ginger
1/4 t. basil
1/4 t. chervil
1/8 t. nutmeg
1 t. salt
1/4 t. fresh ground pepper
4 - 6 chicken pieces, skinned

Pre heat oven to 325°. In large frypan, over medium flame, melt butter. Put flour, spices and herbs into plastic bag and shake. Add chicken, one piece at a time, shake to coat. Add chicken to pan and brown on all sides. Drain chicken on paper towels, then put into baking dish.

STEP TWO

1 large clove garlic, minced
5 mushrooms, sliced
3/4 C. chicken stock
1 T. Worcestershire
1/4 C. dry sherry
4 artichoke hearts, quartered
1 C. sour cream
1/4 C. slivered almonds
2 T. fresh parsley, minced

Add garlic to pan, sauté 2 minutes. Pour off excess butter. Add stock, Worcestershire, sherry and artichokes. Heat through and pour over chicken. Bake, uncovered, for 1 hour. Remove chicken to warmed au gratins. Stir sour cream into sauce and ladle over chicken. Garnish with almonds and parsley.

BIRDS IN BONDAGE

Decidedly kinky! Reserve this one for only your most uninhibited evenings!

1 Hour, 20 Minutes

STEP ONE

4 - 8 boned chicken thighs
(or breasts)
2 C. cooked wild rice (or bread
crumbs)
1/4 C. raisins
1/2 C. walnuts, chopped.

Flatten chicken pieces with mallet or rolling pin. Place equal amounts of rice, raisins and nuts on each piece and roll up, jelly-roll fashion. Secure with thread or toothpicks.

STEP TWO

2 T. butter
1/4 C. water

Heat butter in large fry pan and brown chicken rolls over medium heat. Add water, cover and simmer 15 minutes.

STEP THREE

1/4 C. packed brown sugar
2 T. cornstarch
1/4 t. cinnamon
1 3/4 C. water
1 t. lemon juice
1 t. salt
1/2 C. raisins

Remove chicken rolls to a plate. Mix sugar, cornstarch and cinnamon together, and stir into liquid in pan. Add remaining ingredients and bring to a boil, stirring until thickened. Remove thread or toothpicks from chicken and return to pan. Cover and heat thoroughly.

STEP FOUR

2 T. parsley
2 C. cooked wild rice

Arrange a bed of wild rice in 2 au gratin dishes. Place rolls on a bed of rice, spoon sauce over rolls and garnish with parsley.

Cheese Crock

Get Loose Leaves

Birds in Bondage

Apple Yams

Gerwurtztraminer

Stuffed Grape Leaves

Lettuce Be Lovers

Suite Talk

Apple Yams

Reisling

SUITE TALK

Come up and see me some time!

25 Minutes

STEP ONE

2 chicken breasts, boned, skinned
2 T.butter
1 leek, sliced
2 t. minced fresh ginger
3 T. "Raffeto Chut-Nut" chutney
   or chutney of your choice
1/3 C. Madeira
3/4 C. chicken broth

Melt butter in frypan over medium flame. Add breasts and saute' about 5 minutes per side. Remove chicken to warmed platter, cover. Add leek, ginger, chutney, Madeira and broth to pan, turn flame to high and bring to a boil. Stir constantly until reduced by half.

STEP TWO

1/2 C. whipping cream
salt and pepper, to taste
4 red leaf lettuce leaves
1 T. parsley, chopped
3 T. cashews

Add cream and juices from chicken to pan. Boil until slightly thickened. Season. Lay lettuce leaves on plates, top with chicken breasts, spoon sauce over chicken, sprinkle with parsley and cashews. Serve.

RACY RENDEZVOUS

Get off to a fast start and finish in the first heat!

2 Hours, 45 Minutes

STEP ONE

3 T. butter, room temperature
1 T. parsley, minced
1 T. chives, snipped
1/2 t. marjoram
1 clove garlic, minced
1 T. grated lemon peel
2 - 3 veal cutlets
2 - 3 slices Monterey Jack cheese
2 - 3 slices prosciutto

Blend butter, parsley, chives, marjoram, garlic and lemon peel together. Spread on veal cutlets. Top each cutlet with a slice of prosciutto and a slice of cheese. Roll, starting from small end and tie with string. Refrigerate 2 - 3 hours.*

STEP TWO

1 T. butter
1 T. oil
1/2 C. white wine

In small saucepan, over medium flame, melt butter and oil. Brown veal on all sides. Add wine, cover and simmer 10 - 15 minutes.

STEP THREE

1 T. butter
1/2 bunch spinach (or frozen)
1 clove garlic, minced

Saute' garlic in butter over medium flame for 2 minutes. Add spinach and saute' 1 - 2 minutes. Place in warm au gratin dishes and top with veal rolls.

STEP FOUR

1 T. butter
2 T. pine nuts

Bring flame under wine sauce to high, boil until reduced by half. Add butter and whisk until slightly thickened. Spoon over veal. Sprinkle with pine nuts.

Gratin of Crab

Fast Lane Leaves

Racy Rendezvous

Artichoke Fromage

Gamay Beaujolais

Cheese Crock

Show-Off Salad

Voyeurs Veal

Pistachio Carrots

Gamay Beaujolais

VOYEURS VEAL

will excite the palate and the eye, but be careful . . . your epicurean friend may want to leave the lights on after dinner!

20 Minutes

STEP ONE

2 T. butter
1 C. artichoke hearts
6 mushrooms, thinly sliced
1 T. green onion, sliced
1 T. fresh lemon juice
1 T. parsley, chopped

In large frypan, over medium flame, melt butter and saute' artichokes, mushrooms and onion until onion and mushrooms soften. Add lemon juice and parsley, and turn flame to low while preparing veal.

STEP TWO

1 T. butter
1 T. olive oil
1 t. salt
1 t. white pepper
2 T. flour
1/2 lb. veal cutlets
1 egg
1 T. water

Melt butter and olive oil in large frypan over medium flame. Combine salt, pepper and flour in plastic bag. Add veal and shake to coat. Beat egg and water together in pie pan. Dip both sides of veal in egg. Saute' veal 2 minutes per side and transfer to warmed au gratin dishes. Top with artichoke mixture. Serve.

WOK ON THE WILD SIDE

Live dangerously tonight!

45 Minutes

STEP ONE

1/4 t. sugar
2 t. soy sauce
1 t. fresh ground pepper
2 t. dry sherry
2 skirt steaks, unrolled, cut across
    grain into slices 1 x 1 1/2"
1 t. arrowroot
2 T. water
2 t. peanut oil

Blend sugar, soy sauce, pepper, and sherry with beef. Sprinkle mixture with arrowroot, add 1 T. water and stir until it is too hard to stir, add 1 T. water and repeat process. Let marinate in refrigerator 30 minutes. Remove and blend in oil.

STEP TWO

1 t. arrowroot
6 T. beef stock
2 T. oyster sauce

In small bowl, blend arrowroot, stock and oyster sauce thoroughly. Set aside.

STEP THREE

4 T. peanut oil
3 - 4 cloves garlic, minced
2 T. ginger, cut into matchsticks
4 - 6 green onions, sliced
    diagonally into
3/4 inch pieces
1 T. dry sherry

Heat wok over medium-high flame until smoke rises. Add oil and swirl to coat wok evenly. Add garlic, ginger and onions, stir fry 1 minute. Add beef, stir fry for 1 minute. Add sherry, continue to stir fry while sherry sizzles. Remove beef to bowl as soon as sizzling stops.

STEP FOUR

1/2 lb. snow peas, cleaned and
    blanched
1 8 oz. can whole water chestnuts,
    drained
1 C. cooked white rice
cashews or chopped peanuts

Add 1 T. oil to wok, if necessary. Add snowpeas, stir fry for 2 minutes. Move snowpeas to sides of wok, add well-stirred oyster sauce mixture to wok, as soon as it bubbles, add beef, green onion mixture, water chestnuts, and stir together until blended. Serve over white rice and garnish with cashews or chopped peanuts if desired.

Stuffed Grape Leaves

Roamin' Romaine

Wok on
the Wildside

Pistachio Carrots

Sauvignon Blanc

Artichoke Balls

Romantic Romaine

Affair Nouveau

Carrot Potato Au Gratin

Pinot Noir

AFFAIRE NOUVEAU

Your new affaire can be as hot as you dare, let's sizzle tonight!

40 Minutes

STEP ONE

1/4 C. Port
1/2 C. white wine
1 shallot, minced
1/2 C. chicken stock
1 T. Dijon mustard
1/2 t. chervil
1/2 t. marjoram
1/2 t. tarragon

In small saucepan, over high flame, boil Port, wine and shallot until reduced by half. Stir in herbs, turn flame off, and set aside.

STEP TWO

3 C. chicken stock
2 carrots, sliced diagonally
    into ovals
1 zucchini, sliced diagonally
    into ovals
8 broccoli florets
4 pearl onions, whole

In large saucepan, over medium-high flame, bring stock to a boil. Add all vegetables, except onion, and cook until crisp-tender. Remove to heated bowl. Add onions to pan, boil until tender.

STEP THREE

2 medium beef filets

Prepare a grill or BBQ and grill filets until done as desired.

STEP FOUR

1/2 C. whipping cream

Turn flame under wine mixture to medium, whisk cream in and cook for 2-3 minutes. Place filet in center of warmed plate, place vegetables in clusters around beef. Spoon sauce over beef and serve immediately.

GETTING HOT CHOPS

But don't show it, your partner may get cold feet!

25 Minutes

Step One

1/4 C. soy sauce	Blend cornstarch, soy sauce and water.
2 t. cornstarch	Add pork and marinate while prepar-
1/3 C. water	ing other ingredients, (15-20 minutes).
2 pork loin chips, partially frozen, slice very thin strips ⅛" thick, 2" long	

Step Two

1 T. butter	Heat butter and oil in frypan over
1 T. oil	medium-high flame. Add ginger, garlic,
1 T. minced fresh ginger	and shallot, stir 30 seconds. Drain pork
1 clove garlic, minced	on paper towels, add to pan and stir-fry
1 shallot, minced	until browned on both sides.

Step Three

3 T. grated orange peel	Whisk orange peel and sherry into pan
2 T. sherry	and cook 30 seconds. Add cream and
3/4 C. cream	simmer, stirring frequently until slightly
1 T. snipped chives	thickened. Add mandarin oranges *just*
1/2 C. mandarin oranges	before serving and stir gently to warm through. Spoon mixture into warm au gratins, sprinkle with chives and serve immediately.

Shrimp & Crab Duet

Anticipation Greens

Getting Hot Chops

Pistachio Carrots

Chenin Blanc

Gratin of Crab

Hanky Panky Salad

Papaya Passions

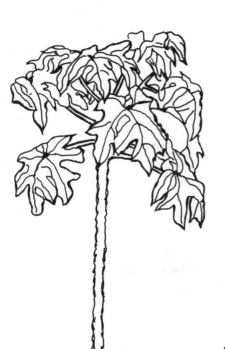

Apple Yam

Reisling

PAPAYA PASSIONS

Don't play under the papaya tree with anyone else but me!

25 Minutes

STEP ONE

1/2 C. flour
1/4 C. water
1 egg, beaten
1 t. salt
1 lb. boneless pork loin, cubed
    and patted dry
peanut oil for frying

Mix flour, water, egg, and salt in bowl. Add pork cubes and toss until well coated. In large frypan over medium-high flame, heat oil and add pork in batches, frying until golden brown on all sides. Remove pork to paper towels to drain.

STEP TWO

1/2 C. water
1/4 C. red wine vinegar
2 T. brown sugar
1/4 C. pineapple juice
1 T. cornstarch
1/2 papaya, peeled, seeded, cut
    into bite size cubes
1/2 C. cashews
2 C. hot cooked rice
1 T. parsley, chopped

In small saucepan, over medium flame, combine vinegar, water, and brown sugar. Bring to a boil stirring frequently. Blend pineapple juice and cornstarch well, stir into vinegar and cook, stirring frequently, until thickened. Gently fold in pork, papaya and cashews. Serve on a bed of white rice. Garnish with chopped parsley.

MAGIC MOMENTS. . .

could be yours tonight, if you get your lover to treat you right!

STEP ONE

2 pieces sourdough or wheat bread, crusts removed
3 T. soft butter

Butter both sides of bread, place on baking sheet. Bake at 350º for 7 - 10 minutes or until golden brown. Place in warmed au gratin dishes.

STEP TWO

1 T. butter
1 clove garlic, minced
5 oz. frozen chopped spinach

Sauté garlic and spinach in frypan over low flame while completing next step.

STEP THREE

1 T. butter
2 lamb noisettes 1 1/4″ thick
   (have butcher prepare for you)

Melt butter in frypan over medium flame. Add lamb and cook turning once, 5 - 6 minutes per side. Remove to warm plate.

STEP FOUR

1 clove garlic, minced
1/2 C. Port
1 t. capers, rinsed and mashed
1/3 C. whipping cream
1/3 C. Roquefort or blue cheese
parsley sprig

Pour off pan drippings, add garlic, capers and Port to pan. Boil over high flame until reduced to about 1/4 cup. Whisk in cream and reduce by half. Whisk in cheese until melted. To assemble: place bread round in warm au gratin, top with spinach, then lamb, nap with sauce, garnish with parsley.

Shrimp
& Crab Duet
Fool Around Salad

Magic Moments

Vegetable Sauté
Merlot

Gratin of Crab

Infatuation Salad

Flashin' Passion

Artichoke Frommage

Fumé Blanc

FLASHIN PASSION

Will you still love me tomorrow?

35 Minutes

STEP ONE

3 T. pecans, toasted and chopped
3 T. butter
2 T. minced onion
1 T. minced mushrooms
3-4 T. rich lamb or beef stock

In food processor, blend pecans, butter, onions and mushrooms 1 minute. Scrape down sides and add enough stock to make a paste.

STEP TWO

1/2 C. rich lamb or beef stock
3 T. red wine vinegar
2 T. port
1/4 C. minced leek
1 T. minced onion
2 T. minced mushrooms
1/3 C. whipping cream
2 T. butter
dash of Tobasco sauce
2 t. bourbon

In large saucepan, combine first 6 ingredients and bring to a boil. Continue boiling until reduced to 2 tablespoons. Add cream and continue to boil until thickened. Turn flame off, whisk in butter. Stir in Tobasco sauce and bourbon. Remove from heat and set in pan of hot water to keep warm.

STEP THREE

4-6 lamb loin chops, well trimmed
  of fat
4-6 pecan halves, toasted salt and
  pepper
2 small clusters of red grapes

Grease rack of BBQ or grill and adjust for medium-high heat.
Bone each lamb chop tying meat from each into a small bundle with cotton string. Rub chops with oil and season with salt and pepper. Grill chops 4-7 minutes per side for medium rare. Spoon sauce into warmed au gratin dishes, top with lamb bundles, garnish with pecan halves and red grape clusters. Serve.

LUCKY IN LOVE

Double your pleasure in the game of love.

1 Hour 20 Minutes

STEP ONE

1 C. dry white wine
1/4 C. plus 2 T. soy sauce
1/4 C. butter
2 T. flour

reserved juice from one 11 oz.
**   can mandarin oranges**
1 t. grated lime peel
2 T. lemon juice
1 t. oregano
1 t. thyme
1 t. ground ginger
1 t. curry powder
1 t. honey

Preheat oven to 400°. In one sucepan over medium flame, combine wine and soy sauce and bring to simmer. In second saucepan over l o w flame, melt butter, whisk in flour and cook 7 minutes. Remove from flame and whisk in wine mixture and reserved juice. Cook over medium flame until thickened. Add remaining ingredients and whisk until thoroughly blended.

STEP TWO

2 game hens, halved
mandarin oranges
parsley sprigs

Arrange hens, skin side up, in large baking pan. Spoon sauce over hens and bake 50 minutes, basting occasionally. During last 15 minutes, add oranges to pan drippings and heat through. Place hens on warm platter, garnish with oranges and parsley sprigs and serve.

Stuffed Grape Leaves

Good Luck Greens

Lucky in Love

Apple Yams

Fumé Blanc

Stuffed
Grape Leaves

Go Fast Greens

Lusty Lapin

Artichoke Fromage

Merlot

LUSTY LAPIN

Rabbits have a habit,
you will too,
we all know what rabbits do!

30 Minutes

STEP ONE

1 T. oil
2 T. butter
1 clove garlic, minced
1/2 rabbit, cut into serving pieces
salt and pepper, to taste

Melt butter and oil in large frypan over low-medium flame. Add garlic to pan, sauté until golden. Season rabbit with salt and pepper. Add rabbit to pan and sauté until browned on both sides.

STEP TWO

1 C. seedless red flame grapes
1/2 C. Port
1/2 C. chicken stock
2 T. minced leek

Combine grapes, port, stock, and leek in small saucepan over medium flame and bring to a boil. Reduce heat and simmer 2 minutes. Remove grapes, turn flame to high and boil sauce until reduced by half.

STEP THREE

2 T. butter
1 t. cornstarch
1 t. tarragon vinegar
2 t. port
salt and pepper, to taste

Blend butter and cornstarch together and add one tablespoon at a time to sauce, blending well. Boil sauce for 1 minute, add vinegar and port, season with salt and pepper. (If sauce is too thick, use a little stock to thin.) Lay rabbit in warm au gratin dishes and spoon sauce over. Serve immediately.

SOMETHING ON THE SIDE

ARTICHOKE FROMAGE

40 Minutes

STEP ONE

1 8 oz. jar marinated artichoke
    hearts, drained
2 T. butter
1/2 onion, sliced
1 leek, chopped
6 mushrooms, sliced
3 cloves garlic, minced
1 T. fresh parsley, chopped
1 T. fresh basil, chopped
    (or 1 t. dried)
1/4 t. fresh ground pepper

Preheat oven to 350°. Butter baking dish. Cut artichoke hearts into quarters. Melt butter in frypan over medium flame, add onion, leek and mushrooms, saute' until soft. Add artichokes, garlic, parsley, basil and pepper. Cook 5 minutes. Pour mixture into quiche dish or shallow baking dish. baking dish.

STEP TWO

1/4 C. mayonnaise
1/4 C. sour cream
2 T. whipping cream
1 T. hot mustard
1/4 C. bread crumbs
1/4 C. parmesan

Blend mayonnaise, sour cream, whipping cream and mustard together, thoroughly in bowl. Spread mixture evenly over artichoke mixture. Mix bread crumbs with parmesan cheese. Sprinkle over top and bake 25 minutes or until golden brown.

APPLE YAMS

1 Hour, 10 Minutes*

1 yam

Add yam to boiling water, cover and cook 30 minutes or until done. Cool slightly, remove skin, cut into slices ¼" or less in thickness.

1 large tart apple, sliced thinly
cinnamon
3-4 T. brown sugar
4 T. melted butter
3 t. brandy

Pre heat oven to 350°. Grease a 9" quiche or pie dish. Alternate layers of apples and yams. Sprinkle each layer with cinnamon, brown sugar, and drizzle with butter. Bake, covered, 30 minutes. Remove cover and continue to bake 40* minutes longer. Sprinkle with brandy just prior to serving.

PISTACHIO CARROTS

10 Minutes

STEP ONE

8 - 10 baby carrots, tops removed, peeled

Steam carrots until just crisp tender.

STEP TWO

2 T. butter
1/2 C. pistachios, shelled
2 T. Triple Sec

Melt butter in small sauce pan over medium flame. Add pistachios and saute′ 1 - 2 minutes. Stir in Triple Sec and remove from heat. Add carrots and toss gently, to coat with sauce. Serve immediately.

CARROT-POTATO AU GRATIN

25 Minutes

STEP ONE

2 carrots, peeled and quartered
2 medium red potatoes, peeled and quartered

Steam or boil potatoes and carrots until tender.

STEP TWO

1 egg
3 T. Parmesan
1 T. butter
1 T. sour cream
1/4 t. dry mustard
pinch cayenne
1 T. Parmesan
1/2 T. butter

Pre heat broiler. Butter a small baking dish or individual ramekins. Mash potato and carrot. Add Parmesan, butter, sour cream, mustard and cayenne. Pureé, using mixer or food processor. Spoon into baking dish or ramekins, sprinkle with Parmesan and dot with butter. Broil 2 - 3 minutes or until golden brown, serve.

VEGETABLE SAUTÉ

15 Minutes

STEP ONE

1 small zucchini, cut into 1″ pieces
2 carrots, cut into 1″ pieces
6 brussel sprouts

Steam vegetables until crisp tender. Cover loosely and keep warm.

STEP TWO

1 T. butter
1 T. olive oil
6 cherry tomatoes
1 T. fresh parsley, minced
1/2 t. basil
1/2 t. marjoram
1/2 t. chervil
2 T. lime juice
2 T. Parmesan

In small frypan, melt butter and oil over medium flame and sauté tomatoes and herbs for 2 minutes. Turn flame to low and add lime juice. Turn all vegetables into warm serving bowl, pour sauce over all. Sprinkle with Parmesan and toss gently. Serve immediately.

INDEX

NAUGHTY NOTES

Never stir soup with your thing.*

* Hot soup!

NAUGHTY NOTES